LITERALLY. BEST. JOKES. EVER.

JOKES for KIDS

CHANELLE GRACE

BroadStreet
PUBLISHING

D1318642

BroadStreet Kids
Racine, Wisconsin, USA

BroadStreet Kids is an imprint of BroadStreet Publishing Group, LLC.
Broadstreetpublishing.com

LITERALLY.BEST.JOKES.EVER.

© 2017 by BroadStreet Publishing®

ISBN 978-1-4245-5503-1
ISBN 978-1-4245-5546-8 (ebook)

Content compiled by Chantelle Grace.

Design by Chris Garborg | garborgdesign.com
Editorial services by Michelle Winger | literallyprecise.com

Printed in the United States of America.

17   18   19   20   21   22   23   7   6   5   4   3   2   1

Author Bio

CHANTELLE GRACE is a witty wordsmith who loves music, art, and competitive games. She is fascinated by God's intricate design of the human body. As she works her way through medical school, she knows it's important to share the gift of laughter with those around her. When she's not studying abroad, she makes her home in Prior Lake, Minnesota.

TABLE OF CONTENTS ....

KNOCK KNOCK JOKES

Knock, knock.

Who's there?

Hoo.

Hoo who?

You talk like an owl.

Knock, knock.

Who's there?

Goat.

Goat who?

Goat on a limb and open the door.

Knock, knock.

Who's there?

Lion.

Lion who?

Lion on your doorstep; open up.

Knock, knock.

Who's there?

Dragon.

Dragon who?

Dragon your feet again.

Knock, knock.

Who's there?

Duck.

Duck who?

Just duck!
They're throwing things at us.

Knock, knock.

Who's there?

Toucan.

Toucan who?

Toucan play that game.

Knock, knock.

Who's there?

Wood ant.

Wood ant who?

Don't be afraid. Wood ant harm a fly.

Knock, knock.

Who's there?

Owl.

Owl who?

*Owl good things come
to those who wait.*

Knock, knock.

Who's there?

Safari.

Safari who?

Safari so good.

Knock, knock.

Who's there?

Fleas.

Fleas who?

Fleas a jolly good fellow.

Knock, knock.

Who's there?

Nana.

Nana who?

Nana your business.

Knock, knock.

Who's there?

Laughing tentacles.

Laughing tentacles who?

*You would laugh too,
if you had tentacles.*

Knock, knock.

Who's there?

Cracker.

Cracker who?

*Cracker another bad joke
and I'm leaving.*

Knock, knock.

Who's there?

Honey bee.

Honey bee who?

Honey, be a doll and open the door.

Knock, knock.

Who's there?

Duncan.

Duncan who?

Duncan my cookies in milk.
Can you open the door?

Knock, knock.

Who's there?

Rhino.

Rhino who?

Rhino every knock knock joke there is.

Knock, knock.

Who's there?

Rabbit.

Rabbit who?

Rabbit up carefully; it's fragile.

Knock, knock.

Who's there?

Herd.

Herd who?

Herd you were home, so can you come out?

Knock, knock.

Who's there?

Bee.

Bee who?

Bee at my house at hive-o-clock.

Knock, knock.

Who's there?

Ya.

Ya who?

Actually, I prefer Google.

Knock, knock.

Who's there?

Gorilla.

Gorilla who?

Gorilla me a hamburger, please.

Knock, knock.

Who's there?

Roof.

Roof who?

Roof day. Let me in.

Knock, knock.

Who's there?

Whale.

Whale who?

*Whale, whale, whale,
what do we have here?*

Knock, knock.

Who's there?

Chimp.

Chimp who?

Chimp off the old block.

Knock, knock.

Who's there?

Iguana.

Iguana who?

Iguana hold your hand.

Knock, knock.

Who's there?

Herring.

Herring who?

*Herring some awful
knock-knock jokes.*

Knock, knock.

Who's there?

Sore ewe.

Sore ewe who?

*Sore ewe gonna open
the door or not?*

Knock, knock.

Who's there?

Geese.

Geese who?

Geese what I'm going to do if you don't open the door.

Knock, knock.

Who's there?

Alligator.

Alligator who?

Alligator for her birthday was a card.

Knock, knock.

Who's there?

Bat.

Bat who?

Bat you'll never guess.

Knock, knock.

Who's there?

Howl.

Howl who?

*Howl you know unless
you open the door.*

Knock, knock.

Who's there?

Fangs.

Fangs who?

Fangs for letting me in.

Knock, knock.

Who's there?

Thumping.

Thumping who?

Thumping green and slimy is climbing up your back.

Knock, knock.

Who's there?

Teddy.

Teddy who?

*Teddy is the beginning
of the rest of your life.*

Why did the chicken cross the road?

To get to your house.

Knock, knock.

Who's there?

The chicken.

Knock, knock.

Who's there?

Odysseus.

Odysseus who?

Odysseus the last straw.

Knock, knock.

Who's there?

You know.

You know who?

Exactly.

Knock, knock.

Who's there?

Wendy.

Wendy who?

*Wendy wind blows
it messes up my hair.*

Knock, knock.

Who's there?

Barbara.

Barbara who?

*Barbara black sheep
have you any wool?*

Knock, knock.

Who's there?

Theresa.

Theresa who?

Theresa joke for everyone.

Knock, knock.

Who's there?

Horton hears a.

Horton hears a who?

I didn't know you liked Dr. Seuss.

Knock, knock.

Who's there?

Rita.

Rita who?

Rita book of knock knock jokes.

Knock, knock.

Who's there?

Butter.

Butter who?

Butter if you don't know.

Knock, knock.

Who's there?

Alex.

Alex who?

Alex the questions around here.

Knock, knock.

Who's there?

Lettuce.

Lettuce who?

Lettuce in and you'll find out.

Knock, knock.

Who's there?

Abbey.

Abbey who?

Abbey stung me on the arm.

Knock, knock.

Who's there?

Rhoda.

Rhoda who?

*Rhoda long way to get here;
now open up.*

Knock, knock.

Who's there?

I'm T.

I'm T who?

Oh, you're only 2?
Is your mom home?

Knock, knock.

Who's there?

Avery.

Avery who?

Avery time I come to your house we
go through this.

Knock, knock.

Who's there?

*Well not your parents
because they don't knock.*

WELL THAT'S PUNNY

I'm taking part in a stair climbing competition.

Guess I better step up my game.

My first job was working in an orange juice factory.

I got canned: couldn't concentrate.

A friend of mine tried to annoy me with bird puns...

but I soon realized that toucan play that game.

I used to be a banker...

but then I lost interest.

I'm reading a book about anti-gravity.

It's impossible to put down.

I'd tell you a chemistry joke...

but I know I wouldn't get a reaction.

I relish the fact that you've mustard
the strength to ketchup to me.

Without geometry...

life is pointless.

I went to a seafood disco last week...

and pulled a mussel.

She had a photographic memory...

but never developed it.

Don't spell part backwards.

It's a trap.

A boiled egg every morning...

is hard to beat.

Let's talk about rights and lefts.

You were right, so I left.

In the winter my dog wears his coat...

*but in the summer
he wears his coat and pants.*

A skunk fell in the river...

and stank to the bottom.

A new type of broom has come out.

It is sweeping the nation.

My friend asked me to stop impersonating a flamingo.

I had to put my foot down.

Someone ripped some pages out of both ends of my dictionary today.

It just goes from bad to worse.

I used to be a baker...

but I didn't make enough dough.

The first time I got a universal remote control I thought to myself...

"This changes everything."

I haven't slept for ten days.

That would be far too long.

I've just written a song about tortillas.

Actually, it's more of a rap.

A book just fell on my head.

I've only got my shelf to blame.

Someone threw cheese at me.

Real mature!

I love Switzerland.

*I'm not sure what the best thing
about it is, but their flag is a big plus.*

When I finally worked out the secret to cloning...

I was beside myself.

A pet store had a bird contest...

with no perches necessary.

I wondered why the ball
kept getting bigger.

Then it hit me.

The other day a clown held the door
open for me.

I thought it was a nice jester.

I asked my mom to make me a pair of
pants.

She was happy to.
Or at least sew it seams.

I applied for a job at the local restaurant.

I'm still waiting.

I was going to look for my missing watch...

but I could never find the time.

I've been learning braille.

I'm sure I'll master it once I get a feel for it.

If a judge loves the sound of his own voice...

expect a long sentence.

I just walked past a shop that was giving out dead batteries...

free of charge.

I used to be addicted to soap...

but I'm clean now.

It was an emotional wedding.

Even the cake was in tiers.

Once you've seen one shopping center...

you've seen a mall.

The other day someone left a piece of clay in my house.

I didn't know what to make of it.

I'd tell you my construction joke...

but I'm still working on it.

My grandma is having trouble with her new stair lift.

It's driving her up the wall.

To the guy who invented zero:

Thanks for nothing.

There was a big paddle sale at the boat store.

It was quite an oar deal.

I tried to finish the left-overs...

but... foiled again.

I really wanted camouflage socks...

but I couldn't find any.

I couldn't work out how to fasten my seatbelt.

Then it clicked.

Did you hear about those new reversible jackets?

I'm excited to see how they turn out.

I'm glad I know sign language.

It's pretty handy.

My dog can do magic tricks.

It's a labracadabrador.

Learning how to collect trash wasn't that hard.

I just picked it up as I went along.

My leaf blower doesn't work.

It sucks.

If you need help building an ark...

I Noah guy.

This boy said he was going to hit me with the neck of a guitar.

I said, "Is that a fret?"

ROFL RIDDLES

I'm light as a feather, but even the strongest man cannot hold me for more than five minutes.

What am I?

Breath.

Mr. Smith has two children. If one of the children is a boy, what are the chances the other is a boy?

50%.

When is homework not homework?

When you do it at school.

What stays put when it goes off?

An alarm clock.

Alexa gets into the shower, gets out, and realizes her hair isn't wet.

How is this possible?

She didn't turn on the water.

What is sticky and brown?

A stick.

What are two things you can't eat for breakfast?

Lunch and dinner.

Without fingers, I point.
Without feet, I run.

What am I?

A clock.

How many apples grow on a tree?

All apples grow on trees.

Does a pound of gold or a pound
of feathers weigh more?

They both weigh a pound.

What has a single eye, but cannot see?

A needle.

Is an older one-hundred dollar bill
worth more than a newer one?

*Of course it is. A $100 bill is worth
more than a $1 bill.*

You throw away the outside, eat the
middle, and throw away the inside.

What is it?

Corn on the cob.

I am an instrument that you can hear,
but cannot see or touch.

What am I?

A voice.

Two people were born in the moment,
but have different birthdays.

How does this happen?

*They were born
in different time zones.*

I can be used to build castles,
but I crumble in your hands.

What am I?

Sand.

I'm in everybody, but everyone still
wants me. I can't feed you,
but I can feed a tree.

What am I?

Water.

A cowboy rode to an inn on Friday. He stayed two days and left on Friday.

How is this possible?

His horse's name was Friday.

You can easily touch me, but not see me. You can throw me out, but not throw me away.

What am I?

Your back.

If you're looking for some food, I know what to do. But if you don't like the cold, I'm not for you.

What am I?

A fridge.

What month do people sleep the least?

February, because it's the shortest month.

You are my brother, but I am not yours.

Who am I?

Your sister.

What kind of room has no windows
or doors?

A mushroom.

The more you work, the more I eat.
You keep me full, I'll keep you neat!

What am I?

A pencil sharpener.

I'm very easy to get into,
but very hard to get out of.

What am I?

Trouble.

The more I dry, the wetter I become.

What am I?

A towel.

A man is twenty years old,
but has had only five birthdays.

Why?

He was born on Leap Year Day.

I go up but never come down.

What am I?

Your age.

A man is sitting in a cabin in Michigan.
Three hours later he gets out of his
cabin in Texas.

How is this possible?

He's a pilot in the cabin of a plane.

If a white house is white and a yellow house is yellow, what color is a green house?

A greenhouse is one that holds plants; it's usually clear.

Can you name three consecutive days without using the words Wednesday, Friday, or Sunday?

Yesterday, today, and tomorrow.

I bring you down but never up.

What am I?

Gravity.

Two fish are in a tank.
One says to the other,

"Err... so how do you drive this thing?"

THINK ABOUT IT...

If you're waiting for the waiter to bring you food,

are you the waiter?

If a dog gave birth to puppies near the road,

would it be cited for littering?

If you dream in color,

is it a pigment of your imagination?

If a clock is hungry,

does it go back four seconds?

If you crash a car on purpose,

is it still an accident?

Why do noses run,

but feet smell?

Is sand called sand because

it's between the sea and the land?

If we can't see air,

do fish see water?

If I work as Security at the Samsung store,

does that make me guardian of the galaxy?

If I hit myself and it hurts,

   am I weak or strong?

Why are they called apartments

   if they are built together?

Who put the alphabet

   in alphabetical order?

If a dog chews shoes

   whose shoes does he choose?

Would a cardboard belt

   be a waist of paper?

TRICKY TITLES

I Love Wills

> by Benny Fishery

Stop Arguing

> by Xavier Breath

Falling Trees

> by Tim Burr

Monkeys

> by Bob Boone

Why Cars Stop
  by M.T. Tank

Turtle Racing
  by Eubie Quick

I Love Crowds
  by Morris Merrier

The Yellow River
  by I. P. Freely

A Great Plenty
  by E. Nuff

Mosquito Bites
  by Ivan Itch

My Lost Causes
by Noah Veil

Flooring
by Lynn O'Leum

Highway Travel
by Dusty Rhodes

It's a Shocker
by Alec Tricity

I Hit the Wall
by Isadore There

I Hate the Sun
by Gladys Knight

He Disappeared
    by Otto Sight

I Didn't Do It!
    by Ivan Alibi

Life in Chicago
    by Wendy City

Without Warning
    by Oliver Sudden

Desert Crossing
    by I. Rhoda Camel

Candle-Vaulting
    by Jack B. Nimble

Happy New Year!
   by Mary Christmas

You're Kidding!
   by Shirley U. Joked

Webster's Words
   by Dick Shunnary

Those Funny People
   by Joe Kur

Winning the Race
   by Vic Tree

Crocodile Jealousy
   by Ali Gator

Fun Games
by R. Kade

I Need Insurance
by Justin Case

Whatchamacallit
by Thingum E. Bob

I'm Someone Else
by Ima Nonna Muss

It's Contagious!
by Lucas Measles

The Great Escape
by Freida Convict

Breaking the Law
by Kermit A. Krime

Cooking Spaghetti
by Al Dente

Proper Housekeeping
by Lotta Dust

Mountain Climbing
by Andover Hand

Poetry in Baseball
by Homer Un

I Love Mathematics
by Adam Up

Exercise on Wheels
by Cy Kling

Stringed Instruments
by Viola Player

Open Air
by Alf Resco

Smash His Lobster
by Buster Crabbe

In the Arctic Ocean
by Isa Berg

Modern Tree Watches
by Anna Log

Forbidden
by Nada Loud

Snakes of the World
by Anna Conda

The Housing Problem
by Rufus Leeking

Artificial Clothing
by Polly Ester

More for Your Money
by Max Amize

Two Thousand Pounds
by Juan Ton

Overweight Vegetables
    by O. Beets

Mineralogy for Giants
    by Chris Tall

Bring to the Store
    by Shaw Ping List

Almost Missed the Bus
    by Justin Time

My Life in the Gutter
    by Yves Trough

Things to Cook Soup In
    by Stu Potts

Tyrant of the Potatoes
  by Dick Tater

I Hate Monday Mornings
  by Gaetan Oop

The Fall of a Watermelon
  by S. Platt

Military Defeats
    by Major Disaster and General Mayhem

Judging Fast Food
  by Warren Berger

I Lost My Balance
  by Eileen Dover and Paul Down

House Construction
> by Bill Jerome Holme

Kangaroo Illnesses
> by Marcus Wallaby, M.D.

Irish Plants
> by Phil O'Dendron

Musicals
> by The Okay Chorale

A Whole Lot of Cats
> by Kitt N. Caboodle

Working with Diamonds
> by Jules Sparkle

Laws of Suffering
   by Grin and Barrett

Errors and Accidents
   by Miss Takes and Miss Haps

Where to Find Islands
   by Archie Pelago

French Overpopulation
   by Francis Crowded

I Like Weeding Gardens
   by Manuel Labor

Who Stole a Cookie?
   by Howard I. Know

Are We There Yet?

> by Miles Away

The Excitement of Trees

> by I. M. Board

A Bundle of Laughs

> by Vera Funny

Artificial Weight

> by Andy Gravity

Fifty Yards to the Outhouse

> by Willy Makit

Foot Problems of Lumberjacks

> by Paul Bunion

Where are the Animals?
by Darryn de Barn

Walking to School
by Misty Bus

The Number Game
by Cal Q. Later

Deep in Debt
by Owen A. Lot

Robotics
by Cy Borg

Bungee Jumping
by Hugo First

Taking Tests
by B. A. Wiseman

Computer Memory
by Meg A. Byte

The Membership List
by Ross Terr

All About Flowers
by Chris Anthymum

The Lost Scout
by Werram Eye

How to Eat Cereal
by Peor A. Bowl

Green Vegetables
> by Q. Cumber

Neat Shirts
> by Preston Ironed

Unclean!
> by Phil Thee

How to Overcome Stress
> by R. E. Lax

I'm Exhausted
> by Rhonda Marathon

How to Succeed in School
> by Rita Lott

Uncooked Soup
by Rob Roth

How to Apply Makeup
by Rosie Cheeks

The Squeaking Cupboard
by Rusty Hinge

Imitating Mozart
by Sam Fony

All Alone
by Saul E. Terry

Let's See That Again
by Schlomo Replay

Circle Perimeter

by Sir Cumference

Deceleration

by Sloane Down

Don't Sit

by Stan Dupp

Some Like It Sweet

by Sugar Kane

Bad Cow Jokes

by Terry Bull

Talkative

by Terry Yaki

Keep them in Suspense
  by Toby Continued

Bad Beverages
  by Travis Tea

Untied Sneakers
  by Tyrone Shoelaces

Why Won't the Car Move?
  by Vlad Tires

Woman in Danger
  by Warner Quick

Bad Gardening
  by Wilt Ed Plant

It Wasn't Her
> by Zoe Didit

The Arctic Oceans
> by I. C. Waters

Together for a Year
> by Annie Versary

The Old Tapes
> by Cass Ette

Throw It Away
> by D. Sposable

Favorite Pizza Toppings
> by Pepe Roni

Third of Five

by Quinn Tuplet

Find Another Lonely Heart

by Q. Pid

BIBLE BELLY LAUGHS

Who was the greatest female
businessperson in the Bible?

> *Pharaoh's daughter. She went down
> to the bank of the Nile and drew out
> a little prophet.*

Who is the shortest person in the Bible?

> *Bildad the Shuhite (shoe-height).
> Nehemiah (knee-high-miah) was a
> close second.*

When was meat first mentioned
in the Bible?

> *When Noah took Ham into the ark.*

How long did Cain dislike his brother?

As long as he was Abel.

At what time of day was Adam created?

A little before Eve.

Where is the first math homework problem in the Bible?

When God told Adam and Eve to go forth and multiply.

Why did Noah have to discipline the chickens on the Ark?

Because they were using fowl language.

Where is medicine first mentioned in the Bible?

When God gave Moses two tablets.

What's the best way to study the Bible?

You Luke into it.

What kind of man was Boaz before he married Ruth?

He was Ruthless.

Who was the greatest comedian in the Bible?

Samson. He brought the house down.

Which servant of God was the biggest lawbreaker in the Bible?

Moses. He broke all ten commandments at once.

Which area of Palestine was especially wealthy?

The area around Jordan. The banks were always overflowing.

Which Bible character had no
earthly parents besides Adam and Eve?

Joshua, son of Nun.

Why didn't they play cards on the Ark?

*Because Noah was standing on the
deck.*

Why couldn't Jonah trust the ocean?

*Because he knew there was
something fishy about it.*

Did Adam ever have a date with Eve?

No, just an apple.

Where was Solomon's temple located?

On the side of his head.

Where is the first tennis match

mentioned in the Bible?

> *When Moses served on Pharaoh's court.*

What did Adam say on the day before Christmas?

> *It's Christmas, Eve!*

How does the Apostle Paul make his coffee?

> *Hebrews it.*

Why didn't Noah go fishing on the Ark?

> *Because he only had two worms.*

How do we know Peter was wealthy?

> *By his net income.*

Who was the smartest man in the

Bible?

Abraham. He knew a Lot.

Who was the fastest runner
in the race?

Adam was the first in the human race.

What animal couldn't Noah trust?

The cheetah.

On the Ark, Noah probably got milk
from the cow. What did he get from
the ducks?

Quackers.

Where is the first baseball game
in the Bible?

In the big inning. Eve stole first and

Adam stole second.

Why didn't Cain bring God an acceptable offering?

Because he wasn't Abel!

Why couldn't they have apples on Noah's Ark?

Because everything was in pears.

How many people went on the Ark before Noah?

Three. The Bible says, "Noah went forth."

Why did the bees take so long to get out of the Ark when the doors finally opened?

They were in the archives (ark-hives).

What kind of lights did Noah use
during night?

Floodlights.

AROUND THE HOUSE

What kind of coat can only
be put on wet?

A coat of paint.

What time is it when an elephant sits
on your fence?

Time to get a new fence.

What turns into another story?

A spiral staircase.

What constantly eats,
but is always hungry?

A fire.

What is covered in holes,
but can still hold water?

A sponge.

What goes up and down the stairs
without moving?

Carpet.

What type of dress can't you wear?

An address.

What always goes to bed
with its shoes on?

A horse.

Why are teddy bears never hungry?

They're always stuffed.

What type of house weighs the least?

A lighthouse.

Why can't a bicycle
stand up on its own?

Because it is two tired.

How do you have a party in space?

You Planet.

How do you make antifreeze?

You steal her blanket.

What did the steak say to the beef?

So, we meat again.

Who gets rid of eggs?

The eggs-terminator.

What jumps from cake to cake and smells of almonds?

Tarzipan.

What cheese is made backwards?

Edam.

What goes up when rain comes down?

An umbrella.

Have you ever tried to eat a clock?

It's very time consuming.

What tastes better than it smells?

Your tongue.

ANIMAL ANTICS

What side of a cat has the most fur?

The outside.

How do dog catchers get paid?

By the pound.

What's another type of key that can't open a door?

A donkey.

Where do fish keep their money?

A riverbank.

What kind of fish chases a mouse?

A catfish.

What do they call pastors in Germany?

German Shepherds.

What animal needs to wear a wig?

A bald eagle.

What do you get if you cross a snake and a lego set?

A boa constructor.

How do snails talk to each other?

By using shell phones.

What's the best way to stop
a charging bull?

Take away its credit card.

Why did the man buy a donkey?

*He thought he might
get a kick out of it.*

What do you get when you cross
a snowman with a vampire bat?

Frostbite.

Why did the kid throw the butter
out the window?

To see the butter fly.

Why did the canary sit on the ladder
to sing?

It wanted to reach the high notes.

Where do mice park their boats?

At the hickory dickory dock.

Where do orcas hear music?

At the orca-stra.

Why do giraffes take so long
to apologize?

*It takes them a long time
to swallow their pride.*

What do you do if a dog chews up
your dictionary?

Take the words out of his mouth.

Why do cows wear bells?

Because their horns don't work.

What do you call an alligator who steals?

A crookodile.

Why did the lamb cross the road?

To get to the baaaarber shop.

What has four legs and says,
"Oom, oom?"

A cow walking backwards.

What do you call a pig who knows karate?

Porkchop.

What do you get when you plant a frog?

A croak tree.

How is a dog like a phone?

It has collar ID.

What would happen if pigs could fly?

The price of bacon would go up.

What do whales eat?

Fish and ships.

What do sardines call a submarine?

A can of people.

What do fish take to stay healthy?

Vitamin sea.

What's a shark's favorite sandwich?

Peanut butter and jellyfish.

Why don't bears wear shoes?

What's the point? They'd still have bear feet!

What do you call a dog
that likes bubble baths?

A shampoodle.

What kind of cars do cats drive?

Catillacs.

What do camels use to hide
themselves?

Camelflauge.

What do you call an untidy hippo?

A hippopotamess.

What do you call a cow that twitches?

Beef jerky.

What's a lion's favorite state?

Maine.

What do cats like for breakfast?

Mice krispies.

What is a horse's favorite sport?

Stable tennis.

What game do elephants play
when riding in the car?

Squash.

Where do horses live?

In the neigh-borhood.

What happened when 500 hares got loose downtown?

Police had to comb the area.

Where do sharks come from?

Finland.

How many skunks does it take to make a big stink?

A phew.